pick the right wine every time

# pick the right wine every time

*Chris Losh*

RYLAND
PETERS
& SMALL

LONDON  NEW YORK

First published in the United States in 2005
by Ryland Peters & Small
519 Broadway, 5th Floor
New York, NY 10012
www.rylandpeters.com

10 9 8 7 6 5 4 3 2 1

Senior Editor  Clare Double

Picture Research  Emily Westlake

Production  Sheila Smith

Production Manager  Patricia Harrington

Art Director  Gabriella Le Grazie

Publishing Director  Alison Starling

Library of Congress Cataloging-in-Publication Data

Losh, Chris.
  Pick the right wine every time / Chris Losh.
    p. cm.
  ISBN 1-84172-968-X
  1. Wine and wine making. I. Title.
  TP548.L6855 2005
  641.2'2--dc22
                              2005004177


Printed in China

# contents

# INTRODUCTION

Wine is the most versatile of drinks. It's your companion at home in front of
the television, an ice-breaker at parties, and a gift for those you want to impress.
It's something to be treated with reverence and with abandon, a drink for every
budget and every occasion.

Why? Because wines, like people, have very different personalities, which is
both their attraction and their curse. On one hand, the variety on offer makes
wine more stimulating, varied, and fascinating than any other drink on the
planet; on the other, with such a lot of choice it can be very easy to Get It Wrong.

The biggest difficulty nowadays is not so much getting a half-decent bottle
(standards are far higher than they used to be), but in getting the right type of
wine for the situation. Here, again, wines are like people.

You probably wouldn't want to receive investment advice from a party animal
or be stuck in a bar with someone who talked about tax refunds all night, but put
the accountant in his office and the reveler in his bar, and they come into their
own. Well, so it is with wine. Take a perfectly good bottle and serve it at the wrong
time or with the wrong food, and it might taste horrible, but get it in the right
place at the right time and it will shine.

That's why this book is arranged not by wine style, but the way that most of us
buy wine: by event. Whether it's a bottle for midweek glugging or Sunday lunch,
a cookout or a blowout, the intention is to cut through the mystery and find wine
styles that fit in with the way you live your life. There's nothing in here about
magnificent Bordeaux châteaux or the history of winemaking in Australia; just
practical information designed to help you get the most out of wine without
spending a fortune.

After all, wine might be stimulating and fascinating, but we don't need to make
things any harder for ourselves than they already are.

PICK RIGHT at home

# WEDNESDAY NIGHT SUPPER

**KEEPING IT FRESH**

*Quite often I visit friends' houses to see half-drunk bottles with the cork stuck back in the top. Bad idea. If you only want to drink a couple of glasses from a bottle (understandable during the week), buy a vacuum set. This involves putting a rubber stopper in the top of the bottle and removing the air with a small pump. It's cheap, easy to use, lasts forever, and will keep your bottles fresh for a couple of days.*

Wine isn't just a special-occasion drink any more. With the possible exception of breakfast, it's a civilized accompaniment to more or less any meal you fancy, and the midweek couple of glasses are ever more popular.

For school nights, I'd suggest finding wine styles that will go with several dishes. That way, if you only drink a couple of glasses on one night, you've still got something left for the next day (see Keeping it Fresh, left).

Chardonnay, for instance, is a wonderfully versatile white. If it's not too heavily oaked, it'll go with fish, chicken, pork, and most pasta dishes. The same goes for other fleshy whites such as Pinot Blanc and Chenin Blanc. Sauvignon Blanc, on the other hand, might be a good match with fish, salad, and some oriental cuisines, but because it's lighter and more aromatic, it can struggle with white meats. Likewise Pinot Grigio.

For reds, mid-weight wines like Pinot Noir and Rioja can work with everything from pasta to meaty fish, pork chops, and even chili. The same goes for young, unambitious Bordeaux. But open a big Cabernet Sauvignon or Shiraz, and, unless you drink it all in one sitting, it could be hanging around for a while. (I'm assuming here that you don't eat steak five nights a week!)

Because midweek food rarely takes more than half an hour to prepare, adjust your wine budget accordingly. Really cheap stuff might actually detract from your meal, but there's no point spending more than you have to. Chile, Argentina, and Portugal are good sources of decent, value-for-money reds; Australia and South Africa for whites.

A good addition to the midweek kitchen is bag-in-box wine. It might not look pretty, but a three-liter box is usually cheaper than four bottles, you can have as much or as little as you want at a time, and the wine will stay fresh for several weeks.

# FRIDAY NIGHT TV WINE

Friday night is the waiting room on the journey to the weekend. What you want is a wine that is in tune with your euphoria at having two whole days off, and isn't going to look at you reproachfully if you slug it back without really concentrating. All of this means simple and pleasurable rather than complex. Big, cheerful flavors are in, elegance and restraint are out.

Most wines like this come from places with lots of sun. Australia, California, and Chile are great at making these luscious, up-front wines, jammed with fruit, and they do it, moreover, at good prices. Since the wine is to be drunk mostly on its own, we're looking for wines that don't have tons and tons of "structure"—which means soft tannins for red wines and low acidity for whites. Tannin and acidity might be essential when matching with food (see pages 42–57), but can get in the way when you're just looking for a simple glass of glug.

So for whites I would rule out high-acid varieties such as Sauvignon Blanc or Riesling. Instead, keep your eyes peeled for an Aussie or California Chardonnay or a South African Chenin Blanc, all of which will be as comforting and generous as your sofa's cushions.

For reds I'd steer clear of Cabernet Sauvignon, unless you have a particular favorite. "Cab" is a great grape, but it can have quite strong tannins, which aren't what you want when you're drinking a wine on its own. Go for naturally softer varieties like Shiraz/Syrah or Merlot.

Australia, again, is great for the former, but California, South Africa, and Chile are all doing great Syrah, too. For juicy Merlot, California is your safest bet. If you want something a little bit different, Argentina does some great swigging Malbec. If you simply have to have a Cabernet, go for Chile, which makes the softest, most approachable examples in the world.

**TAKE NOTE OF OAK**

*When it comes to choosing your whites, be wary of how much oak the wine has. Big, creamy examples with lots of toasty, vanilla oak flavors may be initially exciting, but drinking more than one glass can be an effort unless you're very determined!*

# BEFORE AND AFTER DINNER

There are times before a meal when only a beer, martini, or stiff gin and tonic will do. But wine has star performers of its own. Fino sherry, for instance. It's nutty, tangy, intense, and absolutely bone-dry. Served chilled right down, I have yet to find a better match with predinner nibbles, and its lack of bubbles means you won't get bloated.

Talking of bubbles, what about champagne? Yes, it's a bit of a splurge, but cheaper sparkling wines can do a reasonable job for less-special occasions—just make sure the wine you choose is dry (or *brut* in French).

In summer a fresh, chilled white like a Riesling, Muscadet, or Sauvignon Blanc can be a refreshing intro to a meal, and has the advantage that it might well carry on happily with the food.

But I'd think twice before serving red wine before a meal. It can swamp your taste buds and whatever food is coming next. If you've got fairly flavorsome nibbles, a chilled dry amontillado sherry (absolutely gorgeous—rich, nutty, and tangy) is a classy option and won't spoil if you leave it open for a few weeks.

When it comes to drinks after a meal, you're looking at the opposite end of the flavor spectrum. Instead of dry and light, you're looking for sweet and rich—the equivalent of a soothing massage for your palate rather than pre-exercise stretches.

Oddly, some sweet wines can be almost too unctuous on their own, and need food—Sauternes is a case in point—but those with a naturally higher acidity such as German Riesling (*Auslese* or *Trockenbeerenauslese* (TBA)) are a good post-dinner treat.

Sweeter champagnes used to be hugely popular and are a suitably decadent end to an evening. But for most people the traditional last wine is a fortified: Madeira or sweet sherry (occasionally) or, more likely, a port. Ruby ports are the cheapest, but late-bottled vintages (L.B.V.) or tawnies give far more bang for your buck. Vintage port has undeniable class, but you need to know how to serve it (see below). All ports work with cigars to a degree.

## DECANTING VINTAGE PORT

*Vintage port is unfiltered, which means it has sediment in the bottle. To make sure this doesn't end up in your glass, you need to decant it. Leave the bottle to stand upright for a couple of hours to settle, then pour it very slowly into your decanter (or pitcher if you don't have one) a few hours before serving.*

*If you carry out this process over a candle or a light, you'll see the sediment start to gather at the shoulder of the bottle. When it's about to come over the shoulder and down the bottle's neck, stop. There'll probably be half an inch of port left in the bottle.*

# BARBECUE

The joy of most barbecues is their ad hoc nature—the relaxed feel of eating outside coupled with the chance to pile your plate high with all manner of foods. Both these elements will have an effect on the sort of wines you serve.

Let's take the "outdoors" bit first. What you want to drink if it's lunchtime and baking hot is different if it's seven in the evening and starting to cool off. Generally speaking, the hotter it is, the more attractive those light, refreshing white wines are going to seem.

So if it's hot, look for bottles with plenty of fresh, spritzy acidity and not too much weight. Sauvignon Blanc is perfect, but so are Riesling, Muscadet, Soave, and unoaked Chardonnay. Just make sure you keep the bottles chilled.

These wines might not, strictly speaking, be perfect with the food, but they're perfect with the weather, and if you're serving salads, fish, or even chicken, they'll be OK.

As it cools off, so red wines become more appealing, but it's unlikely ever to be cold enough for you to want huge reds with high alcohol and enormous mouth-drying tannins. Soft, luscious examples like Pinot Noir, Merlot, Chilean Carmenère, Rioja, Malbec, or Beaujolais are a good bet.

When it comes to matching with food, the eclectic nature of barbecue food makes an across-the-board match impossible. How can you get a single wine that will go with salad, chicken, pork chops, and steak?

This is why I wouldn't get too hung up about the wine and go for general rather than perfect matches. Mid-weight whites like Chenin Blanc, lightly oaked Chardonnay, Sémillon, Verdelho, or Viognier will work with everything but red meat. Mid-weight reds like Merlot, Argentine Malbec, Barbera, Grenache, southern French reds like Fitou, and young Rioja will be fine with pork, lamb, burgers, and even chicken up to a point. Zinfandel can be good, too, but it tends to be high in alcohol, so be careful if it's really hot.

Save the bigger, more "classic" reds for formal sit-down barbies, but even here I wouldn't go for anything too heavy unless it's fairly cool (or you're eating indoors).

## COOKOUT TIPS

- Rosé wines, chilled right down, are perfect for the barbecue. Served cool, they are as crisp and refreshing as whites, but take on more weight as they warm up. Make sure they're dry.

- Some reds work really well chilled, too. Beaujolais, Loire Cabernet Francs, and Pinot Noirs are the classics.

- Alcohol with sun is a potent combination, so make sure you offer plenty of water. One glass of water for every glass of wine is about right.

- No need to spend big with barbies. The food is fun rather than classy, so budget accordingly—maybe just above your Wednesday night wine.

# SUNDAY LUNCH

Sunday lunch (or dinner) is something of an in-between occasion. It's several steps up from the rush and bustle of midweek dinners, yet not as involved as a gastronomic blowout; the sort of meal that you want to feel is a bit special, but not one you want to spend all day preparing.

Happily, treating yourself a bit with your choice of wine is one of the best ways of instantly generating a feeling of indulgence without any real extra effort. I'm not suggesting that you bankrupt yourself, but adding 50 percent to what you spend on a midweek bottle should make a significant difference to the quality.

Trading up is a particularly good idea with your Sunday lunch, because good wine shows particularly well when it's not fighting with dozens of huge flavors in the food. And, since typical Sunday lunches are roasts, then by their very nature—solid food that's easy to prepare and simply served—they are fabulous for showing off a better-than-average bottle of wine. If you're going to buy one bottle of decent wine a week, make it for Sunday lunch.

## Chicken and pork

Both of these are at home with either whites or light reds. For characterful whites, it's hard to beat Burgundy with its fascinating Chardonnays. The trouble is that the best wines (though gorgeous) are expensive, while the cheaper versions are rarely worth the money. So, if in doubt, spend a bit extra!

Australia and New Zealand both do some flavorsome (and increasingly elegant) Chardonnays, while Aussie Semillon is a good mouth-filler. If you're having white meat with creamy sauce, a bottle of Riesling is a great and characterful match. Australia's are the best of the New World, but my preference would be for a dry wine from Alsace if you can find it.

If you fancy a red wine with your white meat, Pinot Noirs like red Burgundy (same rules on price apply as for white Burgundies) are best. Otherwise, go for a light- to mid-weight Italian red like Valpolicella or Chianti.

## Lamb

A juicy Spanish red from Rioja or Ribera is a classic combination, but the meat also goes well with red Bordeaux and Chianti. Again, paying a bit extra makes a big difference to the quality, so if you go Spanish look for *reserva* (or *crianza*) on the label to prove it's had a bit of love and attention.

## Beef

Here you need the heavyweights of the wine world: big Cabernet Sauvignons and Merlots or Syrah/Shirazes. A decent bottle of Bordeaux has the most class, but if you want plenty of sweet blackcurrant fruit, Cabs from Chile, Argentina, South Africa, Australia, New Zealand, and California are all worth a look as well.

For Syrah/Shiraz, Australia and the Rhône are classic areas. The former tend to be bigger and richer, and work well if you're having intensely flavored game such as venison.

## Stews and casseroles

Look for cheerfully chunky red wines from the Douro in Portugal or the Côtes du Rhône or Châteauneuf-du-Pape in France. Aussie Grenache, Spanish Garnacha, and Italian Primitivo are decent bets, too.

PICK RIGHT **on special occasions**

# DINNER PARTY

There are different levels of dinner party—from the relatively informal "friends around" to the full-on five-star bash that takes weeks to plan and days to prepare. The way you approach your wine depends on how special the occasion is.

What is true, though, is that these are occasions when going the extra few yards, not just in the level of the wines you serve, but also in the variety of bottles on offer, makes a big difference.

First, the groundwork—getting the quantity right. Each bottle holds six glasses of wine. So if there are four of you, assume that you'll need one bottle for the starter and two bottles for the main course. Next, are you having sparkling wine to start? Dessert wine? Port? If so, the first two will need chilling, while the latter may need decanting (see page 15).

When it comes to the level of wines served, this too depends on the occasion. I wouldn't ever go below the Sunday lunch level. And if it's a long-lost cousin visiting from Australia, you'll need to show it's a big deal with at least one really good bottle.

The good news (for your budget at least) is that if you're serving two bottles of wine with the main course, they don't both have to be superstars. In fact, having one great wine and one good one can make for an interesting exercise in "compare and contrast"!

For sheer class, it's hard to beat the great areas of Europe: Bordeaux, Burgundy, Chianti, Rioja, and Barolo (for reds) and Burgundy, Alsace, and the Loire (for whites). At the mid- to upper price levels, the Rhône, south of France, Chile, South Africa, southern Italy, and Australia all offer good value for money. I'd suggest one wine from each group.

## WHAT TO TAKE

*As a guest, start by asking your host what the meal is and taking something that might go with that. If they prefer not to tell you, assume that your wine won't be drunk that night and take them something of a quality that will at least do for a Sunday lunch (see pages 18–19).*

*Don't, whatever you do, take them something cheap and cheerful—whichever way you look at it, it's an insult. Better to take good chocolate than bad wine.*

## DINNER PARTY TIPS

• Serve your wines properly, which means chilled for whites and (if possible) decanted for reds.

• A bottle of sparkling wine to start with really gives an evening a lift and needn't be that expensive.

• When it comes to buying a bottle of something a bit special, try your local independent merchant rather than a supermarket. Tell them your budget and the occasion, and they'll probably get you something fantastic.

# WEDDINGS AND ANNIVERSARIES

Making a success of big events like these depends on two things: one, making sure that there's plenty of fizz; and two, that it's drinkable.

This might sound like an exercise in the blindingly obvious, but it's amazing how many big events run out of reception sparkly after one glass, or expect their guests to toast the happy couple with something resembling fizzy floor-cleaner.

For the reception sparkler, you'll need something dry. If you go for champagne, look for *brut* (dry) or "extra dry" (just off-dry, confusingly) on the label. For after-dinner toasts, find something sweeter (*demi-sec*).

But unless you have a huge budget, I'd skip champagne. Yes, at the top level it's gorgeous, but at the lower end it's rotten value for money. Instead, try a premium cava (a good one should still be less than half the price of champers), a fizz from the New World (New Zealand is a particularly good source), or a bubbly from France that's not from the

## IT MAKES SENSE TO DO IT YOURSELF

*Supplying your own wine allows you to serve decent wine at a good price. Most venues mark up a wine by around 300 percent, but many charge a relatively small corkage fee for every bottle of yours that they have to open.*

*Rates vary, but even if you pay $12 a bottle, which might double with corkage, you'll have a decent wine that's likely to be better than anything you can get on the wine list at the same price.*

*Corkage on sparkling wines is higher (usually twice the price), but the principle is the same. Do the math. You know it makes sense.*

hallowed Champagne region. *Crémants* from Burgundy, Alsace, and the Loire can be really good value for money.

A bit of market research is essential before buying big volumes, so make sure you try out all your prospective candidates. Tasting a dozen bottles with friends will be a fun night as well as worthwhile, believe me!

When it comes to the meal wines, follow the same rules as for a Wednesday night and look for something that's soft, fun, and palate-friendly at a decent price. Chile, South Africa, south of France, southern Italy, and Argentina should all be on your radar.

Incidentally, if you're buying half a dozen cases of wine from one place, you should be able to negotiate yourself a pretty good discount—don't be afraid to try!

As for amounts, I'd allow half a bottle of sparkly per person and about the same of wine for the meal. Thus, for ninety guests, I'd buy 48 bottles of sparkling wine, maybe 36 bottles of red wine and 24 of white.

Remember, no guest ever complained that there was too much wine, but they'll always grumble if there's too little.

# THANKSGIVING

With its riot of flavors and textures at the dinner table, Thanksgiving is a time of exuberant abandon for your palate, which can be both a liberation and a curse when it comes to getting the right wines.

## Pre-dinner fizz

If you really want to start the day with a bang, champagne or Buck's Fizz is a decadent start. For Buck's Fizz (champagne and orange juice), I'd just use any cheap sparkling wine. If you want your fizz neat, go for a non-vintage *brut* (dry) champagne or a New World sparkler (New Zealand's are good).

## The dinner

If you're looking for the perfect "silver bullet" match for turkey with cranberry sauce, stuffing, and sweet potatoes, forget it—there isn't one. The flavors (from sweet through savory) are just too diverse—and that's before you get into the optional extras like ham and ribs.

Now, while that does mean that you can't plonk one bottle down on the table and expect it to do the whole meal, it also takes a lot of the pressure off the event. Since there's no such thing as an across-the-board match, you can serve your guests a number of different wines and let them make up their own minds about which they like the most. It gives you the chance to stir up a bit of debate when it comes to your selection.

Your best bets for Thanksgiving matches are at the light-to-medium end of the red spectrum and the rounded, flavorful end of the white. For classic red matches, we're looking at Pinot Noir/red Burgundy or a decent Beaujolais. If you try the latter (and it's a good match), try to get one of the "crus" from a village like Fleurie, Morgon, or Moulin-à-Vent. They'll have more concentration than just an ordinary Beaujolais.

You can also try lighter examples of Syrah/Shiraz. Probably not the powerful, inky versions from Australia, but more flowery, red-fruited examples from northern Rhône areas like Crozes-Hermitage or New World countries like Chile or South Africa can work nicely.

Of course, if you want to be patriotic, then the uniquely American Zinfandel has the advantage not just of flying the stars and stripes, but also working pretty well with Thanksgiving fare. White Zinfandel will be too sweet, but the red version will be fine. Just keep an eye on the alcohol levels. Since it frequently gets up around the 15 percent mark, don't expect sparkling post-dinner conversation if your guests have gone through a couple of bottles.

When it comes to whites, look for dry Riesling or Chardonnay. Fumé blanc (an all-American version of Sauvignon Blanc) is a slightly lighter alternative.

If you want to keep it local, seek out the whites from Sonoma County or the Central Coast, which are more elegant than those from the Central Valley.

## TOP TIPS

• Don't get hung up on looking for the perfect wine match. Just make sure there are plenty of different bottles on offer.

• Given the rustic nature of the food, you don't need to go crazy on the quality. Sunday lunch level and slightly above is fine.

• Don't serve huge heavy wines unless you want your guests to fall asleep.

• Yes, it's good to fly the flag and serve some American wines, but this is a good chance to branch out a bit as well, so don't waste it!

# PARTY

To an extent, the best advice I can give for party wine is "make sure there's plenty of it." But I'd also like to qualify that statement by adding, "do make sure that it's drinkable."

If you stock up with the cheapest stuff you can find, it'll probably still be there afterward and you'll have to drink it yourself over the next months. If in doubt, find the cheapest wine on offer, add 30 percent to the price, and don't buy anything below that.

Before charging off to the store, it's worth asking yourself the following questions to help you formulate a plan of attack.

- Is it the sort of occasion (say, moving into a new house) that might require some form of celebratory fizz?
- Is it a hot-weather party or a cool-weather one? In hot weather people tend to drink more white wine.
- Will there be food or not—and what sort will it be? A big vat of lasagne, for instance, is likely to see people reaching for the reds.
- How many people are coming and how much are they likely to drink? Unless your friends are dipsomaniacs, allowing one bottle per person will be more than enough, particularly given that many, if you are lucky, may bring a bottle.

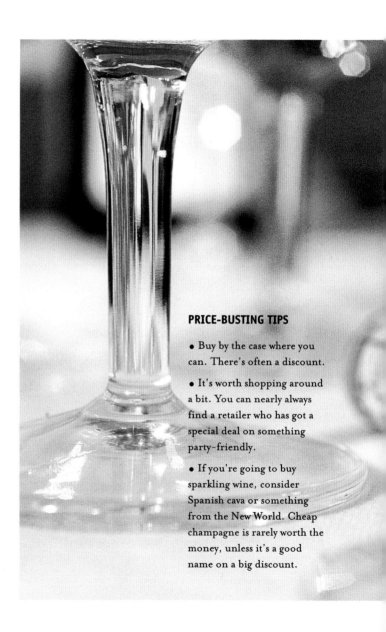

**PRICE-BUSTING TIPS**

- Buy by the case where you can. There's often a discount.
- It's worth shopping around a bit. You can nearly always find a retailer who has got a special deal on something party-friendly.
- If you're going to buy sparkling wine, consider Spanish cava or something from the New World. Cheap champagne is rarely worth the money, unless it's a good name on a big discount.

Your answers should allow you to figure out how much wine you want to buy and, roughly, the proportion of red and white you'll need. After that, it's on to the styles.

Essentially, for parties, you want wine that is similar to that for Friday night (see pages 12–13): simple, undemanding, with a decent whack of fruit, and not too high in either tannin or acidity. Something, in short, that slips down easily.

For whites, New World Chardonnay is a good choice (even with a fair bit of oak), as are South African Chenin Blanc, California Fumé Blanc, Aussie Semillon, or Riesling and Viognier.

For reds, you want opulence without heavy tannin. Portuguese reds are frequently a good budget option, but Shiraz/Syrah, Malbec, and Chilean Carmenère are also safe bets. If you simply have to have Cabernet, stick with the New World, but in my experience most cheap Cabernet is too high in tannin to be pleasurable on its own.

Incidentally, since parties tend to get hot, it's worth filling your bathtub with ice and water and keeping all your wines in there, not just the whites.

PICK RIGHT out and about

# BARS AND PUBS

Boy, does this chapter have to cover a lot of ground! From swanky specialist vinothèques through glitzy bars to spit-and-sawdust pubs, you can get wine of some description in all of them, but how to avoid the rubbish?

## Three basic rules

Take your cue from your surroundings. If it looks like the sort of place that serves six bottles of wine a year, the stock isn't likely to be either fresh or well kept, so drink something else.

If it's a really good specialized wine bar, the staff may have a few good recommendations of their own, so ask them.

Keep your eyes peeled for promotions. Rather than ones that are encouraging you to drink more (a good way of offloading cheap stock), go for promos that cut the price of an expensive wine to an affordable level.

## Choosing a wine

- Generally you want soft, fruit-forward, easy-to-drink wines rather than "classical" clarets and Chablis, which have more tannins (red) or acidity (white).
- I usually find white wines easier to drink in bars, provided they're not too warm. New World Chardonnay is a decent white choice, though some cheap examples can be a bit sickly, so avoid the bottom-end stuff. Sauvignon Blanc is a refreshing palate-sharpener on hot days, but is usually too acidic for more than one glass, so be prepared to switch unless you want indigestion. White Bordeaux (a blend of Sauvignon Blanc and Sémillon) can be easier on the stomach.
- Great by-the-glass whites for me are Riesling, Gewürztraminer, or Tokay Pinot Gris from Alsace, but they aren't always easy to find. Pinot Grigio, the Italian version of Pinot Gris, is more common (and varies from fun and sprightly to thin and nasty, so pick with care).
- If you go the red route, New World Cabernets, Merlots, and Shirazes are soft and juicy, but also get rather heavy for repeat drinking. Spanish reds (Tempranillo or Monastrell) or lighter Italians (Barbera and Valpolicella) are a good alternative. As, believe it or not, is Beaujolais if it's a decent example.

# HOT DATE

This is arguably the hardest of all the categories to get right, since its success depends as much on your attitude as the actual wine you order. That's why it's really important to talk to your date about their preferences before you order. They may well not have strong opinions either way, but it really helps to know if, say, they don't like Chardonnay.

Once likes and dislikes have been safely worked out, it's on to deciding how much to spend. This, in a sense, is the tough bit. After all, we are all capable of ordering a less-than-brilliant wine from a wine list, but if we do it by choosing the cheapest on the menu, then we can fairly stand accused of being stingy.

So without bankrupting yourself, I suggest trawling the wine list at a slightly higher level than you would usually. As a general rule of thumb, take the price of the house wine, double it, and add a bit. At that level you should still be some way below the super-expensive wines (which could lay you open to charges of being flash), but safely into some pretty good stuff.

At this price, the wine ought to speak for itself, but even if it's a bit disappointing, you can hardly be blamed. Having sought a consensus on what to choose at the start and then spent a decent amount on trying to achieve it, you can squarely be said to have done your best. And on a hot date you can't really ask for anything more.

## IF YOU'RE GOING CLASSICAL, DO YOUR HOMEWORK

*Ordering Old World classics like Bordeaux and Burgundy can impress, but it helps to know which vintages or producers to go for—and you don't want to be lost in silent contemplation for ten minutes at the start of your date.*

*If you know the restaurant you're going to beforehand, check out their wine list and do some research. (Heck, you can even take the list into a local wine store and ask them for help!) Either way, a bit of forward planning can help.*

**DO**

*Start your date by ordering a couple of glasses of good champagne. It instantly gives the evening that special feel—and because of its bubbles, fizz lowers inhibitions more quickly, helping conversation flow.*

**DO**

*Consider more expensive wines from cheaper countries—they tend to be soft, rich, and flavorful. While not always a classic match, they give good bang for your buck and are very likeable.*

**DON'T**

*Buy the cheapest wines on offer, even if your date isn't a wine buff.*

**DON'T**

*Spend ages agonizing over the wine list unless your date is a wine lover.*

# VISITING THE IN-LAWS

Forget Olympic finals or politicians being grilled by an interviewer on live TV, taking a bottle of wine to your in-laws is the definition of having to perform under pressure!

Especially, I might add, if it's one of your early visits. And the bad news is that there's no such thing as a blanket recommendation, either. For instance, you might think a classy bottle of white Burgundy is the perfect present— but it's no good if they only drink red wine from the New World.

Much of the success of an in-laws' wine gift depends on your research, which, if you don't know their personal preferences, means grilling your other half. The information could be as specific as "they like 1990 St-Émilions" or as general as "they don't like white wine." Either way, establish some guidelines before venturing out with your checkbook.

If they have some favorites, then great, you know where to start looking. If they don't have any preferences or don't drink that much wine, then your job is both harder (because the potential choice is vast) but also easier, because, provided what you bring is better than what they're used to, they'll be happy.

For the uncritical family, wines that deliver plenty of bang for your buck are a good bet. A $15 red from Chile, Argentina, or South Africa will get you a lot of rich, silky flavors. Whites are harder, but a creamy Australian Chardonnay usually does the trick, as does a waftingly aromatic New Zealand Sauvignon Blanc.

For in-laws who drink wine more regularly but have no great expertise, the key is to find a wine style they like, then consider spending up to twice as much as they usually would in order to get a wine that is guaranteed to deliver. In this, you'll increase your chances of success if you avoid the supermarket in favor of somewhere with staff who can give you decent recommendations.

When it comes to buying for wine-literate in-laws, there's only one option: go to a specialized merchant and ask them to recommend something in the relevant style.

There are two advantages to this: one, it takes the pressure off you (beyond signing the check) and, two, a good merchant should be able to give you a bit of interesting background info about the wine.

Showing that you've gone out of your way to pick up something a bit interesting is worth many cred points and, even in the unlikely event that the wine doesn't hit the spot, you'll still come out of it well.

# PICNICS

I always think that picnics are a bit like barbecues but without the chaos. For starters, the food will be limited, and so will the amount of wines you can take with you, which makes things a lot easier.

Now there are occasions when only a good, chilled six-pack of beer will do, but equally there are times when wine is not just a good alternative, but even the best choice. If it's a special occasion (say, a birthday treat), then why not push the boat out with a big-name champagne to match. You don't need to go the whole hog and buy vintage champers, but a non-vintage from a top house can really make it an occasion to remember. New Zealand makes some great sparkling wine or, at the lower end, cava from Spain is a fair alternative.

For picnic whites, I'd keep it light and zippy—Sauvignon Blancs, Riesling, Soave, and the Spanish white Albariño are refreshing when drunk outside in the sun. For reds, avoid the heavy stuff. Beaujolais is good chilled and juicily appealing, but young Rioja and Pinot Noir work fine, too. Finally, as with barbecue wines, rosé is a great (and underrated) alternative.

## Picnic extras

These can make all the difference. For instance, you absolutely
have to have a cool box. There's nothing worse than lukewarm
champers or white wine. A chiller sleeve to put around open
bottles isn't a bad idea, either—even for reds if it's really hot.

As for glasses, if you don't have a five-star hamper that will
allow you to transport "proper" glasses safely, see if you can get
some non-glass wine glasses. There's something incredibly
depressing about drinking wine out of plastic stacker-cups,
and even plastic wine glasses are a big improvement.

# GIFTS

As with buying for the in-laws, gifting success depends not so much on spending a fortune as getting a wine that will suit the people you're buying it for.

For instance, while a wine buff isn't likely to be impressed with a $7 bottle of easy-drinking plonk, there's absolutely no point in buying *cru classé* Bordeaux for someone who only ever drinks wine on the sofa in front of the TV.

Likewise, if you're taking wine along to a barbecue, you need to make a decision as to whether the bottle is intended for consumption at the event or as a separate present to be drunk later by the hosts.

In other words, use your knowledge of the recipients and the different sections of this book to tailor your bottle to the occasion on which you expect them to drink it.

Having said all that, rather than the straight practical match, you can go down the luxury-item route by buying less usual bottles like champagne, dessert wines, or fortifieds such as port and sherry.

These make great gifts because people often like them, but tend not to buy them for themselves regularly. The inclusion of these luxury wines turns any meal into an occasion, and they'll probably think of you when they pop the cork.

The best value for money comes from non-vintage champagne from a good name and late-bottled vintage port, which gives real after-dinner class without breaking the bank. Dessert wines—even Sauternes, the pinnacle—are well priced, considering how much work has to go into their production.

## BOTTLE-BUYING TIPS

*Bottles of port and champagne often come in their own carton, which makes them both easier to wrap and also better-looking than a bottle on its own. The same goes for spirits.*

*OK, it's not wine, but if you do decide to buy a bottle of spirits for someone, make sure that they like the style you're buying. A fan of sweet bourbon or cognac, for instance, is unlikely to enjoy a pungent, salty Islay whiskey—and vice versa.*

PICK RIGHT eating out

# NAVIGATING THE WINE LIST

It's perhaps not surprising that so many people find ordering wine in a restaurant a somewhat intimidating experience. But fortunately the nightmare scenario of giant, incomprehensible wine list and snooty waiter happens less and less. Besides, if you follow the suggestions below, you'll stack the odds in your favor.

## Ask the waiter

Far from being aloof, good wine waiters are usually only too pleased to help if you ask them for their suggestions. Tell them what you're all eating, what you generally like, and give them a price, and see what they come up with. Remember, it's their job! Just don't let them talk you into spending lots more than you want to.

## Look for familiar faces

If the restaurant doesn't have a wine specialist and your waiter looks clueless, look for brand names, grape varieties, or even countries that you like to drink on the list.

## Try before you buy

A lot more restaurants are offering a decent selection of wines by the glass. If you try a selection with your appetizers (or before sitting down to eat), you'll be able to order bottles of your favorites with confidence. Single glasses can also be a fantastic way of keeping everyone happy if, for instance, your table of four orders red meat, white meat, vegetarian, and fish.

## Look for clues on the wine list

Nowadays, more and more wine lists have helpful descriptions of the flavors of the wines and even, in some cases, food-matching suggestions. Make the most of them.

## Avoid house wines

The fact that house wines are the cheapest wines on the list doesn't, by any stretch, make them the best value. Typically, they're very, very cheap wines that have been hugely marked up, and I've rarely had even a halfway decent one. My benchmark would be to find the price of the house wine, add 50 percent, and start looking around that level.

## Consider safety first

If you are really struggling, certain wine styles
make good "bale-outs"—not necessarily the
best wines on the list, but solid and reliable.
You won't go far wrong with Chilean Cabernet
Sauvignon, California Merlot, Australian
Chardonnay and Shiraz, and New Zealand
Sauvignon Blanc.

### RESTAURANT MARK-UPS

*These vary significantly from
country to country and from
eatery to eatery, but it's not
unreasonable to expect a
restaurant to triple or even
quadruple the price of a
wine that it's selling. In
other words, if you
habitually spend $10 on a
bottle in the supermarket,
you'll probably need to
spend somewhere around
$30 in a restaurant to get
a comparable quality.*

# FRENCH

The French have a good claim to being the nation that gave great food to the world—and the same could be said when it comes to food and wine matching.

The point about classic French food—unlike, say, Thai cuisine—is that because it's usually a fairly simple mix of ingredients, it is much easier for it to work in harmony with the wine, allowing both to shine at once. So if you're ever going to splash out and spend big in a restaurant, this is the type of food with which to do it.

Obviously, in the suggestions below you could substitute, say, a California Cabernet for a Bordeaux. But I've stuck with French recommendations for two good reasons: French wines are generally very food-friendly; and your average French restaurant doesn't sell many wines from anywhere else!

### Seafood

Oysters, shrimp, and *moules marinière* are absolutely at their best with zingy northern French whites like Chablis, Muscadet, and Sauvignon Blancs from the Loire.

### Fish

Depends how it's cooked. For light, white fish, simply grilled, go with the flinty Sauvignon Blancs of Sancerre. Creamy sauces need something more substantial, like a white Burgundy or an Alsace Riesling. Meaty fish like monkfish can work with lighter reds such as Pinot Noir, decent Beaujolais, or Loire Cabernet Franc, as well as bigger Burgundies.

### Casseroles

If there's wine in the sauce, then it's usually a good bet to use the same wine to accompany the casserole. Thus *coq au vin* and *boeuf bourguignon* both work with simple Burgundy, though the beef can

also stand up to more substantial "comfort" wines, such as reds from the Rhône or the south of France. These dishes are simple, hearty food, so there's no need to spend big on the wine.

## Chicken

In a salad, go with medium-bodied whites like Chablis or simple Burgundy. If it's roasted, find a good wine to show the chicken off, like a decent white Burgundy. If you're eating really good meat (say, *Poulet de Bresse*), red Burgundies work, too.

## Beef

Depends a bit on how it's cooked and how good the cut is. Simple *steak frites* or more rustic joints are good either with cheap Bordeaux, Côtes du Rhône, or southern French reds. For top-quality filet, you want as good a wine as you can afford from Bordeaux, Burgundy, or classic Rhône areas like Côte Rôtie.

## Game

Wines with a bit of age go best with any earthiness in the meat. Again, old Burgundies and Bordeaux are the classic matches.

## Cheese and pâté

Sweet Sauternes is a nailed-on classic match with both foie gras and Roquefort. For big, pungent (or smoky) cheeses, try Gewürztraminer from Alsace; for goat cheese, Sauvignon Blanc is a classic (and classy) pairing. For Brie, Camembert, et al, white Burgundy is your man!

## FRANCE AND HER GRAPE VARIETIES

### WHITES

Loire/Sancerre: Sauvignon Blanc

Burgundy/Chablis: Chardonnay

Bordeaux/Sauternes: Sauvignon Blanc, Sémillon

Alsace: Riesling, Gewürztraminer, Pinot Gris

### REDS

Bordeaux: Cabernet Sauvignon, Merlot, Cabernet Franc

Burgundy: Pinot Noir

Loire: Cabernet Franc

Beaujolais: Gamay

Northern Rhône (Côte Rôtie, Hermitage, etc.): Syrah/Shiraz

Châteauneuf-du-Pape: Grenache

Southern Rhône: Grenache, Shiraz, Mourvèdre

South of France: Grenache, Shiraz, Mourvèdre, Carignan

# ITALIAN

Italian food is justifiably among the most popular in the world. Its riot of colors and flavors, while retaining a suitably down-home feel, makes it a comfort food *par excellence*. It also has the singular advantage of being exceptionally wine-friendly, and most dishes work pretty well even if the wine match isn't perfect.

## Pasta

It's all about the sauce. For seafood-based pasta (*vongole*, for example), you can go with just about any white that doesn't have lots of oak in it. Pinot Grigio will be fine, and so will Sauvignon Blanc, Chablis, or a lightish unoaked Chardonnay.

For aromatic, fragrant pasta sauces like pesto, you need a wine that isn't going to override the flavors. So, gently flavored Italian whites like Gavi or Soave can work, as can a Catarrato from Sicily. Outside Italy, Albariño, New World Riesling, a California

Fumé Blanc, or mid-weight Chardonnays are fine.

For carbonara-type creamy sauces, you need a bit of structure to cut through the cream, but not too much fruit flavor, which may well clash. I'd recommend either the same sort of whites that match the pesto, or lighter reds like a Montepulciano, a cheap Bordeaux, or a Cabernet Franc from the Loire.

For meatier sauces like Bolognese, try the more heavyweight Italian portfolio of reds. Chianti is a good match, but I'd tend not to go for the cheapest. Good Chianti is great, but bad Chianti is a miserable experience, and spending a bit extra can make a big difference. Primitivo, from the south, is a good (and cheaper) alternative. Otherwise, any good, gutsy wine will do: Cabernet Sauvignon, Shiraz/Grenache blends (for example, from the southern Rhône Valley), Zinfandel, or Chilean Malbec. There's plenty of scope to choose your favorite—so go to it!

## Pizza

With its massive mix of flavors, pizza is not an easy dish with which to get an absolutely perfect wine match. But then it's not that kind of food, so don't get hung up on it.

As a general rule, I'd favor wines with gentle rather than in-your-face flavors and of no more than medium weight. Even pizzas with lots of toppings tend not to be heavy, and a big, gutsy red wine will just stamp all over them.

For whites, a fresh, gentle Italian like Soave or an unoaked (and not over-fruited) Chardonnay work with most; for reds, Barbera and Montepulciano (from Italy), a southern French Roussillon or Fitou, or young Rioja are safe bets.

## Other classics

Meaty lasagne and ravioli follow the same rules as Bolognese. For vegetarian versions, take the middle-of-the-road carbonara route. For veal, Soave is the lighter match. If it's served with a heavier sauce, try a Pinot Noir.

# CHINESE

As with all types of food, but especially Asian cuisines, there is no such thing as a "one bottle suits all" match for Chinese food. If you're in a decent-sized group, the best bet is to pick a selection of different bottles and try small amounts of different wines with each dish. If you're there as a couple, you'll probably have to resort to wines by the glass to get really good matches right the way through the meal.

That's the bad news. The good news is that Chinese food does offer some genuinely good matches. Sauvignon Blanc (or champagne, if you're pushing the boat out) works with spring rolls and most seafood dishes, while lusher whites such as Chardonnay or Sémillon go with bigger-flavored chicken or pork dishes. Avoid anything that's searingly dry like Sancerre or Chablis—the sweetness of many Chinese dishes means the wine needs a little weight and lushness to it.

Another advantage of Chinese food is that, while it's usually heavily flavored, it's rarely actually hot, which means that red wines can play more of a part. As with the whites, the natural opulence in most New World wines means they usually make a better match.

Duck dishes are a classy partner with New Zealand Pinot Noir, while staples like beef and black bean sauce work with bigger, sweeter New World wines such as Chilean Carmenère, California Merlot, and Aussie Shiraz.

## THE GEWÜRZTRAMINER CONUNDRUM

*Gewürztraminer is often touted as a good match with Chinese food, but its big, perfume-y flavors mean there's a possibility for hideous clashes, too. If in doubt, ask yourself whether the dish you've chosen will work with a side dish of litchi nuts, Gewürz's signature flavor. If it won't, stick with something more neutral, like Pinot Blanc or Chardonnay.*

# JAPANESE

With its purity of flavor, Japanese food can be one of the easiest of the Asian cuisines to match with wine, particularly if you're having sushi. The Japanese often drink sake with it, and for me the best match is the wine that is closest to sake stylistically: fino or manzanilla sherry, which have a delicate nutty, savory flavor profile and are bone-dry. If you prefer non-fortified wine, the key is to get something dry and even a little austere. New World whites tend to have too much sweetness of fruit for sushi, so you're better sticking to Europe and "classic" regions like Sancerre, Chablis, or Burgundy, where the flavors tend to be flinty and chalky rather than actively fruity.

Meatier Japanese dishes obviously require red wine, but probably not anything too enormous, which might stamp all over the flavors. So, provided what you've ordered isn't too spicy, medium-bodied European reds are likely to be best. Young Bordeaux or Burgundies work well, and so can Chianti, Rioja, and Loire Cabernet Francs. If you want to go New World, a Kiwi or Aussie Pinot Noir (from Tasmania if they've got it) is probably your best bet.

For anything with lots of dominant strong flavors that are "difficult" for wine (for example, Japanese pickles, wasabi, and sesame oil), you might want to go native and try that sake!

## AND FROM LEFT-FIELD...

*If you're looking for something a bit different, dry (brut) champagne can be an inspired match with sushi, particularly if it's a good, chalky blanc de blancs (i.e. made from Chardonnay). For teppanyaki, a rich, lush amontillado sherry can do the trick.*

# THAI

With its myriad spices and penchant for chilis, it's difficult to get a perfect wine match with Thai food. The most important thing is to gauge the heat of the dish. If you crunch down on a green chili, don't expect a glass of dry red wine to bring you much relief. In fact, very few Thai dishes suit red wine, so you can more or less head straight for the white section of the wine list, whatever you're eating.

Why? First, the aromatic nature of the dishes is better suited to the flavor profiles of white grapes. Red wines either override the spices completely or, worse, clash with them. Second, white wines have no tannin, which is a Good Thing (see Tannins and Heat, opposite). Not only that, but what they do have is higher acidity, which can help to freshen your palate and counteract any heat in the dish just as effectively as beer.

A little sweetness isn't by any means a bad thing either, so my top recommendations for Thai food would be German Riesling (Spätlese or Kabinett if they've got it), juicy, aromatic Sauvignon Blancs from New Zealand, and apricot-scented Viogniers. For hot, but light dishes (say pork, chilis, and basil), try a fresh, neutral Soave or Pinot Blanc. For meatier dishes, go with an Alsace Tokay Pinot Gris.

# INDIAN

The biggest problem with matching wine to Indian food comes down to one word: heat. If you are addicted to searingly hot dishes such as vindaloo, you'll just have to accept that your choice is, to put it mildly, limited. But if you prefer creamier or more medium-spiced dishes, then things get easier.

If in doubt, the safest bet for Indian food is, as with Thai, to avoid red wines for reasons of tannin (see left) and look instead at whites. Since the dominant flavor in Indian cooking tends to be the sauce rather than the meat, it's perfectly possible to have red meat and white wine.

There are two routes to go down: either find a big, pungent white that will wrestle with the food head-on (like an Alsace Gewürztraminer), or go for something deliberately more neutral that acts as a "straight man" to the food and soothes the spiciness.

Lush Tokay Pinot Gris or Pinot Blancs (again from Alsace) are good bets here. For creamier dishes like korma or passander, Rieslings are a decent match. For fish curries, New Zealand or South African Sauvignon Blanc work OK. A personal favorite of mine is white Rhône, which can work with many dishes, though it's not always easy to find.

If you fancy something out of left-field, big dessert wines like Tokaj work surprisingly well. They have the lushness to stand up to even pretty hot dishes and plenty of cleansing acidity to keep the mouth fresh. You won't find many on restaurant lists, but if you're entertaining at home they could be a real crowd-pleaser.

## TANNINS AND HEAT

*Tannins cause the mouth-drying sensation (you can feel it on your teeth) that you get in red wine. They're an essential part of red wine's makeup and, usually, an essential ingredient in providing "structure" when it comes to food matching. But because they dry your mouth out they exaggerate any heat in food, so be very wary about ordering any red wine with spicy dishes. If you insist on red, make it a soft one like a Dolcetto, Beaujolais, or Valpolicella.*

# MEXICAN

With its robust flavors and cheerful spices, there's absolutely no point in getting too fancy when it comes to matching wines with most Mexican food. So, unless you're going to a trendy CaliMex fusion restaurant (when things get kind of complicated and your best bet is probably to ask the waiter for help), the key is to keep it simple.

With chunky food like chicken burritos, you're looking at the soft, round, and full-flavored end of the spectrum rather than delicate and aromatic, which leads us once again to Chenin Blanc, Chardonnay, and/or Sémillon country. A bit of oak is fine, but remember that anything that's too heavily wooded will increase any heat in the dish.

For more esoteric seafood fare featuring, say, shrimp, limes, and chili, Rieslings can be an inspired match, and the acidity will freshen your palate as effectively as beer.

For chunky red meat dishes, you need a wine that is not overly

tannic, so that the heat in the food isn't exaggerated. This rules out many Cabernet Sauvignons, but there are still plenty of wines out there with a bit of attitude that work well. Southern French reds (Rhône Villages, Languedoc) have a bit of grunt to them, as does Shiraz.

But, for me, the best match with tortillas, tacos, et al, is California's own Zinfandel. Big and lush, it manages to be spicy without being aggressive, and soft without being flabby. Well worth a look—just don't confuse it with white Zinfandel (a sweetish pink version, made from the same grape).

# GREEK AND LEBANESE

The classic cuisine of Greece and Lebanon features a mixed selection of starters (mezze), followed by a more solid meat or fish course. And the good news is that, with its emphasis on natural ingredients and generally simple, fresh flavors, wine matching is something of a dream with most of them.

Why? Because there aren't too many conflicting flavors to get in the way, and the dominant flavors, garlic and herbs, are far easier to match with wine than, say, chilis and lemon grass.

For mezze, a good, crisp white wine is the best starter. A modern white Rioja or Albariño from Galicia in Spain; a Loire Sauvignon Blanc; a herby Catarrato from Sicily; or a cool Soave—even a crisp Portuguese white—will all work with the majority of Greek and Lebanese starters.

You can even try an unoaked Chardonnay with lamb mezze if they've been drizzled with lemon juice, and the wine could then continue with the main course if you've ordered grilled fish.

For meats, again, the simplicity of flavors makes matching reds comparatively simple. Huge, sweetly fruited wines aren't likely to be a great match with savory, herby flavors, so you are probably best off looking in Europe or cooler areas of the New World. Bordeaux, Rioja, and Ribera del Duero are good, as are Chianti and Fitou. If you want an Aussie Cabernet, try Western Australia.

## GO NATIVE

*There are plenty of good Greek wines appearing now, frequently blending unpronounceable native grapes like Agiorgitiko with more familiar ones like Cabernet Sauvignon. They're worth a look. And if you fancy an established classic, Château Musar from Lebanon has been a powerful, chunky, cult wine for decades.*

# SEAFOOD

While with seafood it's broadly true that if you order anything chilled and white you won't be too far off the mark, there are some matches that are indisputably better than others. After all, there's a world of difference between the delicate flavors of, say, lemon sole and meaty fish like tuna.

Crawfish, shrimp, and the like work really well with very delicate, fresh whites like Muscadet. For simple fish dishes (without strong sauces), you'll never be far wrong with a Sauvignon Blanc, particularly if you shell out a bit extra and get one from Sancerre in France. Fresh and steely, it's a classic match with the likes of sole.

For meatier fish like halibut and sea bass, you need a bigger wine, and, while you can still get away with a good Sauvignon Blanc, a lightly oaked (or unoaked) Chardonnay, like a Chablis, will carry the day nine times out of ten.

For seriously meaty fish like tuna and shark, you want biggish (lightly or unoaked) Chardonnays from countries like Australia or South Africa or even light reds like Pinot Noir, Beaujolais, or Cabernet Franc.

**SEAFOOD TIPS**

*If you're having simple crawfish as an appetizer, why not accompany them with a chilled glass of fino sherry? Elegant, classical—and very Spanish!*

*If you have to pick one "bale-out" wine to go with a variety of different dishes, Chablis is probably your best bet. It's fresh, but with reasonable body.*

# FUSION FOOD

This is some of the toughest food to get a good wine match with. For starters, it's non-traditional, so there are no tried-and-tested classic matches; and its tendency to throw unusual tastes together can make it hard to predict flavors just by looking at the menu.

The good news is that, since most fusion restaurants tend to be fairly serious establishments, they often have a knowledgeable wine waiter—so don't be shy about asking him or her for advice.

Although you can usually come up with something reasonable by a process of elimination (if a dish is Thai-influenced, you can follow the rules on page 52, for example), for me, the key is not to get too hung up on the search for perfection.

Fusion food is fun, and you need to buy into that spirit of adventure. Be like the chef and try stuff out. Think laterally, throw out the rule book—and enjoy yourself!

**ADVENTURER'S TIP**

*A fair few fusion dishes mix big flavors to make an even bigger combination. This can be too much for most wine styles, but sherry (yes, sherry) can work really well for these power-plates if you get the right style. Try manzanilla or fino with fish, amontillado with game, and oloroso with red meat.*

keeping it RIGHT

# STORING

When it comes to eating at home, buying the right wine in the first place is only part of achieving vinous nirvana; you need to treat your new purchase right if you're to get the most out of it.

OK, if you're planning to drink a wine within a week of purchase, then short of storing it in the oven or the freezer it doesn't matter much where you keep it. But any longer than that and it helps to bear the following in mind. Trust me, you'll save yourself a lot of ruined bottles.

## Where to store it

Basically, wine likes the sort of conditions that humans don't: cool, humid, and dark. The ideal temperature is about 50°F (10°C). If you have a cellar, perfect. If not, find a place that checks as many of the boxes as possible.

But (and it's a big but) just bear in mind that big temperature swings are an absolute no-no. So storing it in the garage or under the eaves of the house is out. Better to find somewhere that's dark and a bit too warm but constant—maybe a hallway or under the stairs where it's a steady 60°F (15°C)—than somewhere the temperature fluctuates wildly.

## How to store it

In a word: horizontally. The lapping of the wine stops the cork from drying out.

## How long to store it for

This depends on two things: the environment and the wine itself. The warmer it is, the faster a wine ages, so a bottle that might last a couple of years in a cellar will probably be shot after six months in your living room.

Then there's the question of whether your wine will improve with age, even if it's well kept. Most modern wines (both reds and whites) are ready for drinking straight away and are likely to deteriorate, rather than improve, with time. So if in doubt, pull the cork!

### NOTE

*Fine wines are an exception to this "drink young" rule. See overleaf.*

# SERVING

Serving wine correctly is easy—and doing it well can have a big impact on what it tastes like. The following three variables make a big difference.

## Glass size

Essentially, the bigger the better, since you can slosh the wine around and release its aromas. Titchy wine glasses should be thrown out.

## Temperature

There's a tendency to overchill whites and serve reds too warm. Bad news. White that's too cold loses all its flavors, while a hot red tastes unbalanced and alcoholic. Most fridges are colder than the ideal white wine temperature, so take the bottle out half an hour or so before serving. Conversely, the idea of "reds at room temperature" was established long before central heating, so you might want to leave your bottles in a cooler part of the house (or even outside) before bringing them to the table.

## Decanting

Most reds and even some whites are improved by decanting, since it gets oxygen into them and opens up their flavors. Decant reds several hours beforehand. Whites can be done just before serving. (See page 15 for how to decant.)

# COLLECTING

There are two types of wine collector: those who do it for personal enjoyment and those who do it for profit. They're as different in their *modus operandi* as those who buy a house to live in and those who buy one to rent out.

## Investing

This is a highly involved business and not something you should get into lightly. Sure, there are always figures floating around that if you'd bought Château X ten years ago it would have tripled in value, outperforming the stock market. But there are also likely to be many more wines that barely improved or went down in value over the same period.

In the limited space available here, the best advice I can give is that you treat any company offering guaranteed returns with considerable caution. If in doubt, call one of the established merchants in London, Tokyo, or New York and see if they've heard of them. There are still plenty of scammers out there.

If you want to invest independently, then you'll need to familiarize yourself with the fine wine market of Bordeaux in particular, but also, to a lesser extent, Burgundy, Tuscany, and California. You'll also need to get in with your local fine wine merchants to make sure that

you get the first releases of *en primeur*. This is a long-term project, not a get-rich-quick one.

## Collecting for pleasure

Having a working wine cellar is without doubt the best way to increase your knowledge, enthusiasm, and experience of the subject, and it's not as difficult or expensive as you might think. Fifty wines, for instance, would be a reasonable starter collection, and that's only four cases.

There are two keys to having a successful cellar: first, that you have somewhere really decent to store the stuff; and second, that you balance your stock.

The storage point is perhaps the most important. Once you start buying better wines, they often do improve with time. And if you're going to have wines sitting around for a few years (or decades), they need to be in the right ambience. If you don't have a cellar and don't fancy excavating a small purpose-built one (not so expensive as you might think—check out the small ads at the back of wine magazines), it's possible to buy large wine chiller cabinets, which replicate the effects of a genuine cellar and can stand in your garage.

## STORING TOP WINES

*Should you ever buy really expensive wines, whether for enjoyment or as an investment, you should leave them in a purpose-built warehouse until you decide to drink or resell them. Although it's nice to be able to look at your purchases, these are expensive products and their quality (and value) will be affected should you keep the wine in less than perfect conditions for any length of time.*

As for mixing your stock, the best cellars are practical rather than vinous trophy cabinets. They should contain wines for every occasion, whether it's Tuesday night pasta or a golden wedding celebration, not just be stuffed full of big names to show off to your friends.

You can, of course, build your collection with single bottles, but buying by the case is cheaper and gives you the chance to drink each wine at varying ages so you can find its peak—much more of an issue with good wine than everyday stuff. Buy a case a month for a year, and soon you'll have a really good collection.

The best place to pick up cases is at specialized independent merchants, who will have far more interesting bottles than, say, the supermarket, and at reasonable prices. Get to know them, and before long they'll be approaching you with deals! If you fancy stocking up on older wines, auctions are a good place to look, and you can pick up some real bargains.

# PHOTOGRAPHY CREDITS

**Alan Williams**
Pages 1, 2, 3, 4–5, 6, 12–13,
30–31, 33, 36, 40, 42–43,
44–45, 46, 47, 48–49, 49,
50, 51, 52–53, 55, 56–57,
58–59, 61, 62–63

**Debi Treloar**
Pages 10, 18, 19, 20–21, 23,
26, 34–35

**Ian Wallace**
Pages 16–17, 38–39, 39

**Peter Cassidy**
Pages 8–9, 24–25

**William Lingwood**
Pages 14, 27

**Dan Duchars**
Page 60: wine cellar in
a house in Surrey designed
by Spiral Cellars Ltd
+44 20 8834 7371
www.spiralcellars.com

**James Merrell**
Page 54

**Francesca Yorke**
Pages 28–29

# ACKNOWLEDGMENTS

Thanks to my parents for introducing me to wine at an early age,
to my lovely wife, Bola, who has borne my vinous ramblings
down the years with great good humor, and to my daughter
Rebecca, who makes it all worthwhile.